ICONIC NATIONAL PARKS

JOSHUA TREE NATIONAL PARK

BY YVETTE LaPIERRE

An Imprint of Abdo Publishing
abdobooks.com

Cover image: Joshua Tree National Park is renowned for its unique plant life.

abdobooks.com

Printed in the United States of America, North Mankato, Minnesota.
052025
092025

Cover Photo: Photostock-Israel/Science Photo Library/Getty Images
Interior Photos: Shutterstock Images, 4–5, 26–27, 32–33, 43 (top), 43 (middle), 43 (bottom), 45; Red Line Editorial, 7, 30; benedek/E+/Getty Images, 10–11; Hannah Schwalbe/National Park Service, 13, 36, 39; Robb Hannawacker/National Park Service, 14; Elias Goldensky/Library of Congress, 16; Sierralara/RooM/Getty Images, 18–19; Maggie Kuo/Shutterstock Images, 21; Dennis W. Donohue/Shutterstock Images, 24; Apu Gomes/AFP/Getty Images, 31; Jason Finn/Alamy, 34; Michal Balada/Shutterstock Images, 40; Destination Scenics/Alamy, 42 (top); Andriy Blokhin/Shutterstock Images, 42 (middle); iStockphoto, 42 (bottom)

Editor: Christa Kelly
Series Designer: Marley Richmond

Library of Congress Control Number: 2024948610

Publisher's Cataloging-in-Publication Data

Names: LaPierre, Yvette, author.
Title: Joshua Tree National Park / by Yvette LaPierre
Description: Minneapolis, Minnesota: Abdo Publishing, 2026 | Series: Iconic national parks | Includes online resources and index.
Identifiers: ISBN 9781098297183 (lib. bdg.) | ISBN 9798384919704 (ebook)
Subjects: LCSH: Joshua Tree National Park (Calif.)--Juvenile literature. | Deserts--Juvenile literature. | Natural monuments--Juvenile literature. | Scenic landscapes--Juvenile literature. | National parks and reserves --Juvenile literature.
Classification: DDC 979.4--dc23

CONTENTS

CHAPTER ONE

WHERE TWO DESERTS MEET

Kenna and her family were spending spring break in Joshua Tree National Park. As they entered the park, Kenna got her first glimpse of Joshua trees. They were tall and spikey with twisted branches that reached toward the sky.

The family's first stop was Hidden Valley. Everyone grabbed their water bottles and headed down the short nature trail. Kenna and her sister, Jess, took turns reading the signs along the trail. They learned about

Three-fourths of Joshua Tree National Park is designated wilderness.

the area's wildlife and history. They were surprised that so many plants and animals lived in the desert.

After lunch, Kenna's parents led them to Jumbo Rocks. Kenna got a picture with a rock that looked like a giant skull. Afterward, Jess suggested taking a hike to an abandoned gold mine. As Kenna followed her sister down the trail, she couldn't believe that there was so much to see in the middle of a desert.

JOSHUA TREES AND MORE

Joshua Tree National Park covers 792,623 acres (320,763 ha) of desert in Southern California. It protects an area where two deserts meet. The western end of the park is in the Mojave Desert, and the eastern half is in the lower and hotter Sonoran Desert.

The park is best known for its namesake tree, the Joshua tree. Joshua trees grow only in the Mojave and Sonoran Deserts and the nearby San Bernardino Mountains. The largest trees in the park are 40 feet (10 m) tall.

JOSHUA TREE NATIONAL PARK

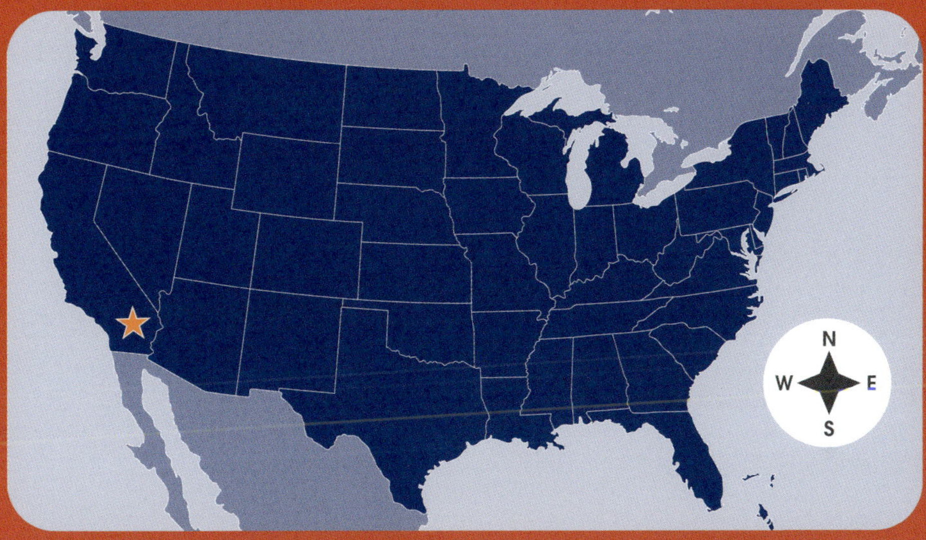

Joshua Tree National Park is ringed by mountains and includes parts of the Mojave and Sonoran Deserts. How do you think this variety of landscapes affects the region's wildlife?

The park features many other wonders too. Colorful cacti, grasses, and wildflowers carpet the desert floor. Rare palm oases dot the landscape. Animals find shade out of the hot sun, adapted to life in the desert.

Joshua Tree National Park is also well-known for its recreational activities. Rock climbers come to the park for its massive boulders and unusual rock formations. Stargazers lie under the night sky to see the park's bright stars. Still others visit the park for its historic sites.

VISITING THE PARK

Joshua Tree National Park's fascinating history and beautiful scenery attract more than three million visitors each year. The park is open 24 hours a day year-round. Inside the park, people can find three visitor centers, a nature center, nine campgrounds, and many picnic areas.

More than 90 miles (140 km) of scenic roads cross the park. Pull-outs with informational signs mark special sites. Visitors can further explore the park on 191 miles (307 km) of hiking and horse trails.

PERSPECTIVES

PARK ECONOMICS

Each year, visitors spend tens of millions of dollars in cities near Joshua Tree National Park. Thousands of jobs have been created to support these visitors. In 2023, the economic benefit of Joshua Tree National Park for the region was $209 million. Former Joshua Tree Superintendent David Smith said, "National park tourism is a significant driver in the national economy . . . and it's a big factor in our local economy as well. We . . . are glad to be able to give back by helping to sustain local communities."

Spring and fall are the most comfortable times of the year to visit. The average temperature during the day is 85 degrees Fahrenheit (29°C). The temperature falls to 50 degrees Fahrenheit (10°C) at night. In winter, the temperature can drop below freezing at night. Summers are very hot and dry. Temperatures can reach above 100 degrees Fahrenheit (40°C) in the middle of the day. The area receives an average of only four inches (10 cm) of rain each year. But no matter the season, the park holds countless adventures for visitors.

RAIN AND SNOW

Joshua Tree National Park is very hot and dry for much of the year. The little rain it gets often comes in short, heavy bursts. Those downpours can cause dangerous flash floods. In the winter, it can hail and even snow. Visitors to Joshua Tree should be prepared for all kinds of weather.

CHAPTER TWO

HISTORY OF JOSHUA TREE NATIONAL PARK

Joshua Tree National Park's history began long ago, when the area was wetter and covered by grass. A river crossed the land. Mammoths and saber-toothed cats roamed the grasslands. Giant ground sloths ate Joshua tree blossoms.

About 10,000 years ago, after the last ice age, the first humans arrived. Today, these early humans are known as the Pinto. The Pinto lived in the park's Pinto Basin. They hunted large animals with spears. Their stone spear

Ancient Pinto artifacts have been found in Pinto Basin.

PERSPECTIVES

DESERT PEOPLES

Joshua Tree National Park is located in the traditional homeland of many American Indian nations. Members of these nations continue to visit places in the park that were important to their ancestors, such as the Oasis of Mara. The park works with tribal governments to help manage and protect the nations' homelands. Exhibits and videos at the park's visitor centers tell the stories of the past and present American Indians of Joshua Tree.

points have been found in the park.

As the area became warmer and drier, more people moved into the region. These people included members of the Serrano, Chemehuevi, Cahuilla, and Mojave American Indian nations. They moved seasonally in search of food. They harvested pine nuts, mesquite beans, acorns, and cactus fruits for food and medicine. They wove baskets and sandals from the tough leaves of Joshua trees. They ground nuts in shallow holes in rocks. These holes, known as mortars, are found in the park's Wonderland of Rocks area.

Visitors can see American Indian art on rocks in Joshua Tree National Park.

STOLEN LAND

White miners began arriving in the Joshua Tree area in the 1800s. They dug mines in search of gold and silver, propelled by the frenzy of the California Gold Rush. Soon, ranchers arrived too. They grazed cattle in the foothills. They rerouted water from rivers into tanks for their animals.

These new activities made life difficult for the American Indians living in the region. White settlers cut off the native nations' access to natural resources, such as food and water. The settlers brought diseases that

Minerva Hamilton Hoyt hired biologists to make reports outlining the importance of the Joshua Tree region. The reports encouraged the government to make the area a national park.

killed many American Indian people. Then they stole what remained of the American Indian nations' land. In the 1860s, the US government forced the nations to leave their homes and relocate to reservations, small pieces of land the government set aside for the nations.

In the early 1900s, Los Angeles and other Southern California cities were growing fast. By the 1920s, new roads were built across the desert. This brought more visitors. Some moved to the area. Many dug up cacti and other desert plants for their gardens. Others destroyed plants and even set fire to Joshua trees.

APOSTLE OF THE CACTI

Minerva Hamilton Hoyt moved to Pasadena, California, in the late 1890s. She soon grew to love the desert near her home. She also loved gardening and native plants. She was worried about the number of desert plants that were being destroyed.

Hoyt spent two decades working to protect desert landscapes. She held exhibitions to educate people about the importance of

MOUNT MINERVA HOYT

Minerva Hoyt passed away in 1945, but her legacy lives on through Joshua Tree National Park. In 2012, a mountain was named after Hoyt to honor her work. Today, visitors to Joshua Tree can climb Mount Minerva Hoyt for views of the desert she loved.

More than 25 percent of the locations in the National Park System were added by Franklin D. Roosevelt.

the desert. She organized groups of gardeners to help spread the word. She began a letter-writing campaign to protect the desert. She even met with President Franklin D. Roosevelt. Hoyt became known as the Apostle of the Cacti.

Her hard work finally paid off. On August 10, 1936, Roosevelt established Joshua Tree National Monument. It protected 825,000 acres (334,000 ha) of desert. In 1994, the monument was declared a national park. This change reflected that the land was being protected for both educational and recreational purposes.

STRAIGHT TO THE SOURCE

Minerva Hamilton Hoyt moved from New York City to Pasadena, California, in the late 1890s. She quickly felt "the call of the desert." She slept in the open desert in a sleeping bag under the stars. Without her devotion, there might not be a Joshua Tree National Park today. She described the desert as:

> *A world of strange and inexpressible beauty, of mystery and singular aloofness which is yet so filled with peace. . . . [The desert] possessed me, and I constantly wished that I might find some way to preserve its beauty.*

Source: Polly Wells Kaufman. *National Parks and the Woman's Voice: A History*. University of New Mexico, 1996, p. 37.

CONSIDER YOUR AUDIENCE

Adapt this passage for a different audience, such as your friends. Write a blog post conveying this same information for the new audience. How does your post differ from the original text and why?

CHAPTER THREE

PLANTS AND ANIMALS

The desert may look dry and empty, but it's teeming with life. Joshua Tree National Park supports more than 800 species of plants. These plants include trees, bushes, cacti, wildflowers, ferns, and mosses. The star of the park is the Joshua tree. Joshua trees can live for hundreds of years. Only one type of moth pollinates the tree's blossoms. It's called the yucca moth.

Joshua trees are essential for the region's wildlife. The trees provide shade and food for

Joshua Tree has so many plants that the original name proposed for the park was Desert Plants National Park.

the desert's animals. One animal even uses the tree as a tool. A bird called the loggerhead shrike hunts small animals and drops them on the tree's sharp blades to kill the prey.

The Joshua tree isn't really a tree. It's a type of yucca, which is a succulent. True tree species in the park include pines, oaks, and ironwood trees.

Joshua Tree National Park is home to 15 species of cacti. Cactus species in the park include silver cholla, teddy bear cholla, Mojave mound, cushion foxtail, and grizzlybear pricklypear.

In the spring, wildflowers cover the desert in a

PERSPECTIVES

JOSHUA TREES

According to one story, Joshua trees got their name when members of the Church of Jesus Christ of Latter-day Saints were crossing the desert in 1853. It was a hot and sunny day. Suddenly, clouds appeared in front of the bright sun. The leader of the group thought the trees looked as if they were lifting their arms to God in thanks for the shade. He decided to name the trees after Joshua, a prophet from their religion.

Desert globemallows are often called apricot mallows due to the flowers' bright orange color.

rainbow of colors. Flowers in the park include yellow desert golden poppies, white ghost flowers, purple royal desert lupine, red Wyoming Indian paintbrushes, pink desert five-spots, blue Mojave asters, and orange desert globemallows.

MAMMALS

Joshua Tree National Park has 57 species of mammals. Coyotes, jackrabbits, white-tailed antelope ground squirrels, and kangaroo rats are found throughout the park. Less commonly seen are foxes, bobcats, bighorn sheep, and mule deer. The park also has 16 species of bats.

Most of the park's animals are active at night. Daytime can be too hot for the animals, especially in the summer. Many dig burrows in the ground. They rest in the shade during the hot summer days. In winter, they huddle within the burrows for warmth.

Though desert life can be difficult, the park's mammals are well adapted. Many have evolved to need little water. Kangaroo rats can survive without ever drinking water. They get water from their food.

REPTILES

Forty-six species of reptiles make their homes in the park. Lizards, such as the desert spiny lizard, can often be seen sunning themselves on rocks. When it's too hot, they hide in cool holes.

Snakes are less commonly seen. There are 26 species of snakes in the park. Of those, seven are species of rattlesnakes.

The desert tortoise, California's state reptile, also lives in the park. These tortoises have been on the earth for 15 to 20 million years. They can live for 15 to 20 years. Desert tortoises were once very common in the park. Unfortunately, their numbers have dropped sharply due to human activities. They are now considered threatened.

COTTONWOOD SPRING OASIS

Some park rangers consider Cottonwood Spring Oasis one of the park's best-kept secrets. The Cahuilla people used the spring for centuries and left clay pots in the area. Miners and ranchers frequently stopped there for water. Today, several hiking trails allow visitors to explore the area. It is one of the best spots in the park for bird-watching.

BIRDS, AMPHIBIANS, AND MORE

More than 250 species of birds have been seen in the park. Some pass through the park on their way elsewhere. Many of these migrating birds are waterfowl, such as ducks, egrets, and herons.

Greater roadrunners can eat poisonous and venomous prey, including rattlesnakes, scorpions, and horned lizards.

Other birds stay in the park seasonally. Juncos, sage sparrows, and western bluebirds are examples of seasonal visitors.

Many birds live in the park all year. Among the most famous of these birds is the greater roadrunner. It can run at speeds of 15 miles per hour (24 kmh) or more when chasing lizards. Other park residents include Gambel's quail, golden eagles, red-tailed hawks, and black-throated sparrows.

Despite how dry Joshua Tree is, it is home to two species of amphibians. The red-spotted toad spends most of its life underground. It appears aboveground only after a heavy rain. The park's other resident amphibian is the California tree frog. This frog lives throughout the park in rocky areas near water.

Other wildlife in Joshua Tree National Park includes thousands of species of insects and spiders. One of the most fascinating insects in the park is the darkling beetle. This insect can go its entire life without a sip of water. The park also hosts more than 75 species of butterflies and even more moths.

FURTHER EVIDENCE

Chapter Three discusses many of the plants and animals that live in Joshua Tree National Park, including the desert tortoise. What was one of the chapter's main points about the tortoise? Watch the video on the website below. Does the information in the video support this point? Does it present new evidence?

DESERT TORTOISE

abdocorelibrary.com/joshua-tree-national-park

CHAPTER FOUR

RECREATION

There is plenty to see in Joshua Tree National Park. Scenic drives provide a good introduction to the park. Roads lead to many of the park's popular spots. These include Cottonwood Spring Oasis, Pinto Basin, and the Wonderland of Rocks area.

Visitors can also explore the park on foot. The park has about 300 miles (500 km) of trails. It's important for visitors to stay on these trails. Going off trail can damage the fragile desert soil and plants.

The drive from the north entrance of Joshua Tree to the south entrance takes about one hour.

The park's shorter trails and nature walks can be enjoyed year-round. The Lost Horse Mine trail has informational signs about the park's natural and human history. Barker Dam Trail explores an area used by early cattle ranchers. Hidden Valley Trail leads to a hidden spot that may have been used by cattle thieves. Cap Rock Trail takes hikers past boulders and Joshua trees.

Visitors should attempt longer trails only in cooler seasons. A popular long trail is the Boy Scout Trail. It leads into the Wonderland of Rocks area. It can take six hours or more to complete this trail.

ROCK STARS

Many people are fascinated by the strange shapes of the rocks in Joshua Tree National Park. Skull Rock looks like it has two sunken eye sockets. Other fun rock formations include Penguin Rock and Heart Rock. More interesting rock formations can be found in the Jumbo Rocks area of the park.

ROCK CLIMBING

Joshua Tree National Park is famous for its rock climbing. It has more than 8,000 climbing routes for beginners through experts. Visitors can take a class or hire a guide to explore the climbing routes safely.

Scrambling is another way to explore the park's large rocks and boulder piles. This is a combination of hiking and climbing over big rocks. Most of the scrambling routes are off marked trails. Some of the easier routes require only good hiking shoes. Steeper routes require hiking and climbing gear.

PERSPECTIVES

STAYING SAFE

Exploring Joshua Tree National Park can be exciting, but it can be risky too. The park's rangers provide many tips to help visitors stay safe. One of their most important recommendations is to bring plenty of water on hikes. Hikers should drink water when they feel thirsty and rest when tired. Maps are important too. It is easy for visitors to get lost, especially when they are hot and thirsty. Every year, park rangers have to rescue visitors from the park's trails.

STARGAZING

Joshua Tree National Park is one of the world's International Dark Sky Parks.

PARK VISITORS BY MONTH

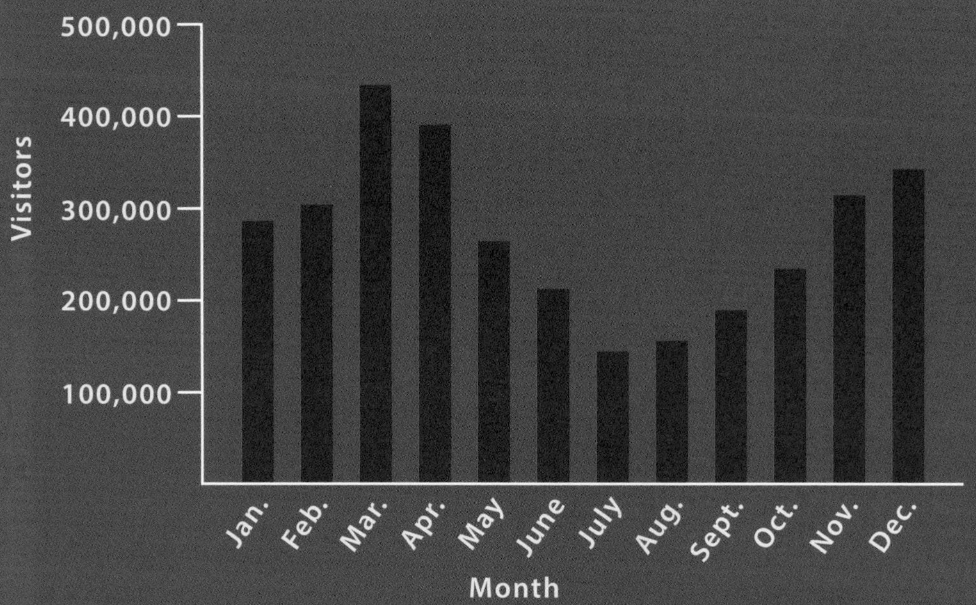

This bar graph shows the number of people who visited Joshua Tree National Park each month in 2023. Which months had the most visitors? Which had the fewest? Why do you think some months or seasons have more visitors than others?

On clear and moonless nights, stargazers can see countless stars. The park is also a fantastic spot for viewing meteor showers.

Visitors can stargaze from any dark place in the park. However, the park has four designated stargazing areas. Park rangers recommend stargazing in the Quail Springs, Hidden Valley, Cap Rock, and Ryan Mountain

Joshua Tree frequently hosts ranger programs to teach visitors about the night sky.

parking lots. These parking lots have minimal light pollution.

EXPLORE ONLINE

Chapter Four explores some of the recreational activities visitors to Joshua Tree National Park can enjoy. One of these activities is stargazing. Read the tips on the website below. What new information did you learn about stargazing?

STARGAZING IN JOSHUA TREE

abdocorelibrary.com/joshua-tree-national-park

CHAPTER FIVE

CARING FOR THE PARK

Though Joshua Tree National Park has long been a desert, the park has been getting hotter and drier over the past 100 years. This is mostly due to climate change. Also known as global warming, climate change is the global rise in temperatures due to human activity. This rise in temperatures causes other negative effects, including more frequent droughts and wildfires.

Since 1895, the average temperature in Joshua Tree National Park has risen by almost

Climate change is impacting Joshua Tree's plants, animals, and visitors.

In the hottest areas of the park, there are more dead Joshua trees than living trees.

three degrees Fahrenheit (2°C). Annual rainfall has decreased by 39 percent. These changes have resulted in more wildfires and the decline of Joshua trees and other native species.

FEWER JOSHUA TREES

Joshua trees are feeling the stress of climate change. Biologists have found fewer young trees growing. Joshua trees need moist ground to sprout and survive. Experts warn that if temperatures continue to increase as expected, most or all of the Joshua trees in the park will die from heat and drought.

Many desert species will suffer if Joshua trees decline or disappear. Yucca moths and other animals depend on Joshua trees for food, shelter, and shade. These species are also affected by the rising temperatures themselves. Many are not adapted to the climbing heat. If the rise in temperatures continues, some species will have to move to cooler areas. Others will die.

DECLINING SPECIES

The desert bighorn sheep is one species that has declined due to climate change. The sheep's habitat in the park is becoming too hot. As the desert warms, the sheep will need to move to

JOSHUA TREE REFUGES

As the climate continues to warm, 80 percent or more of the park could become too hot and dry for Joshua trees. The trees may have a better chance of survival in higher areas that are cooler and receive more rainfall. Park rangers are working with experts to identify and protect these areas.

In 2024, Joshua Tree park rangers used radio transmitters to track 15 desert tortoises.

higher, cooler places outside the park. If they don't, their populations will continue to fall.

Desert tortoise populations in the park are declining too. The species' population is falling due to climate change, habitat loss, and disease. Researchers estimate that 80 percent of the park will not be able to support tortoises if temperatures continue to increase.

Birds are also suffering due to climate change. For the past century, many species have been disappearing from Joshua Tree and the larger Mojave Desert. Surveys report a 43 percent decline in bird species. This is mostly due to climate change and habitat loss.

Biologists are working hard to save the park's plants and animals. They work with other experts to learn more about how changes in the climate impact wildlife. They also work to educate the public on ways climate change can be managed.

PERSPECTIVES

DESERT TORTOISE TRACKERS

Since 2003, biologists have been attaching small radio transmitters to the shells of desert tortoises in Joshua Tree National Park. The transmitters send signals that biologists can track to learn more about the tortoises' behavior. By watching the signals, scientists can tell when tortoises are active, how far they travel in a day, and where they go. Biologists use the information they gather to help protect the tortoises.

FIRE

Joshua trees and other park life are increasingly threatened by wildfires. More than a million Joshua trees died when the nearby Mojave

National Preserve caught fire in August 2020. The wildfire killed countless more cacti, bushes, shrubs, and native grasses.

Fires have always been a part of the Joshua Tree landscape. But warmer, drier conditions have led to more frequent fires. In addition, non-native plants act as fuel for fires. This causes fires to spread faster than before. After a fire, more non-native plants sprout.

To help prevent fires, park staff are removing non-native grasses and shrubs. They are also cutting back plants around Joshua trees to protect the trees from future fires. The park issues campfire bans and restrictions when the risk of fire is high.

SMOG

Joshua Tree National Park is not far from Los Angeles and other major cities. Smog blows into the park from these cities. In fact, Joshua Tree has some of the dirtiest air of all national parks. Many days, air pollution levels are unhealthy for park visitors and rangers.

Unlike rangers at many other national parks, rangers at Joshua Tree National Park put out all fires, even those started naturally, in order to protect the park's fragile desert environment.

Air pollution is unhealthy for the park's native plants and animals too. Chemicals in the pollution help non-native plants grow. Small particles in the dirty air also make the air hazy, so it can be hard to enjoy the views in the park. Climate change adds to these problems. Smog becomes worse in the heat, further decreasing visibility in the park.

Joshua Tree National Park's unique beauty makes it one of the most visited national parks in the United States.

Despite the many challenges facing the fragile desert ecosystem, Joshua Tree National Park rangers are working tirelessly to protect the park. One of their main goals is to reduce the effects of climate change. The park is using more solar power and electric vehicles to reduce pollution that contributes to global warming.

Rangers also educate visitors on the causes and effects of climate change. This encourages visitors to do their part to protect the local ecosystem. Together, park staff and tourists can protect the plants, animals, and landscapes of Joshua Tree National Park.

STRAIGHT TO THE SOURCE

In 2019, the Center for Biological Diversity petitioned the State of California to list the Joshua tree as a threatened species. In the petition, researchers at the Center argued:

> *The Joshua tree has long been the most iconic species of the Mojave Desert. . . . It has recently become [a symbol] of our society's failure to address the climate crisis. But the Joshua tree is also uniquely situated to become an example of successful action to save a species threatened by climate change. Action taken in and by California to save the species can serve as a model for proactive climate adaptation efforts not just in California but around the world.*

Source: *A Petition to List the Western Joshua Tree (*Yucca brevifolia*) as Threatened under the California Endangered Species Act (CESA)*. Center for Biological Diversity, 15 Oct. 2019, biologicaldiversity.org. Accessed 8 Oct. 2024.

WHAT'S THE BIG IDEA?

Take a close look at this passage. What is the main connection being made between Joshua trees and climate change? How could saving the species impact the rest of the world?

PARK LANDMARKS

Black Rock Canyon is in the northwest corner of the park. It features a campground, nature center, and juniper tree forest.

Skull Rock is a rock formation. Rain eroded the big granite boulder until it resembled a skull.

The **Oasis of Mara** is one of the few places in the park with natural fresh water. The oasis is surrounded by palm trees, bushes, and grasses.

Cholla Cactus Garden is known for its rare plants. It's a popular place to enjoy the sunrise and sunset in the park.

Hidden Valley Nature Trail is a one-mile (2 km) hike. Signs along the trail provide information about the natural and human history of the area.

Keys View is a popular lookout. It provides sweeping views of the Coachella Valley.

STOP AND THINK

Tell the Tale

Chapter One of this book explores one family's experience at Joshua Tree National Park. Imagine you and your family are taking a trip to Joshua Tree. Write 200 words about the sites you want to see. Why are these sites important or interesting? Why do you want to visit them?

Surprise Me

Chapter Three describes some of the plants and animals that live in Joshua Tree National Park. After reading this book, what two or three facts about Joshua Tree's wildlife surprised you? Write a few sentences about each fact. Why did you find each fact surprising?

Say What?

Studying national parks can mean learning a lot of new vocabulary. Find five words in this book you've never heard before. Use a dictionary to find out what they mean. Then write the meanings in your own words and use each word in a new sentence.

Take a Stand

Chapter Two discusses Minerva Hamilton Hoyt's campaign to protect the desert and its plants. She spent many years writing letters and meeting with people to persuade them to create a park in the desert. Is there a place that is important to you? Why is it important? How would you persuade people to care about this place?

GLOSSARY

apostle
a dedicated follower of a person or cause

biologist
a scientist who studies the natural world

economic
relating to money

ecosystem
a community of organisms living together and interacting

habitat
the natural home of a plant or animal

oasis
a place in the desert with water

prophet
a member of a religion who delivers messages that are believed to come from a god or divine being

pull-out
an area on the side of a road where drivers may stop to view an area of interest

smog
air pollution that reduces visibility

succulent
a plant that has thick, fleshy parts for storing moisture

threatened
in danger of no longer existing

ONLINE RESOURCES

To learn more about Joshua Tree National Park, visit our free resource websites below.

Visit **abdocorelibrary.com** or scan this QR code for free Common Core resources for teachers and students, including vetted activities, multimedia, and booklinks, for deeper subject comprehension.

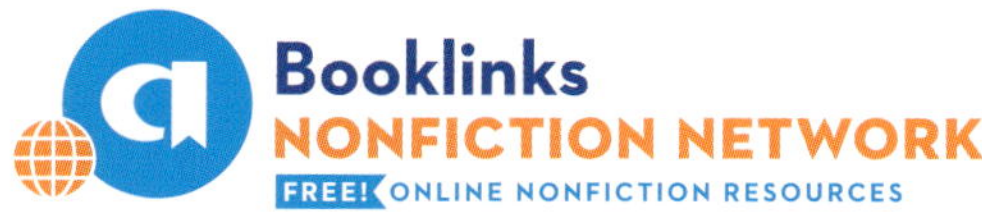

Visit **abdobooklinks.com** or scan this QR code for free additional online weblinks for further learning. These links are routinely monitored and updated to provide the most current information available.

LEARN MORE

Alexander, Heather. *Only in California*. Wide Eyed, 2022.

USA National Parks. DK, 2024.

INDEX

About the Author

Yvette LaPierre grew up in the Mojave Desert. She enjoys hiking in Joshua Tree, Death Valley, and other desert parks. She currently lives in North Dakota and is the author of more than 30 books for young readers.